You've dreamed and wished it; now your dream is real. Explore the bliss of life with a unicorn through these original, hand-drawn illustrations.

Carve out some time, grab your pens, a big handful of Skittles and get coloring.

This is chill time. Day dream to your heart's content.

There's plenty of space to test your color combos in the back pages. Plus each illustration is repeated so you get double the fun.

When your masterpiece is finished you can cut them out, frame them, stick them on your wall.

Have fun and keep coloring.

Original Illustrations by Kate Gillett
for unicornista.com

ISBN: 978-0-9954131-0-8

Want a better life? Find yourself a unicorn

With your own unicorn you'll eat cupcakes for lunch

You'll always be able to charge your phone

And get to the front of every queue

Your unicorn will know all the best dance moves

And where you left that other sock

Though your unicorn will never let you win at X-Box

They will help you choose the best shoes

When you fart in yoga class your unicorn will take the heat

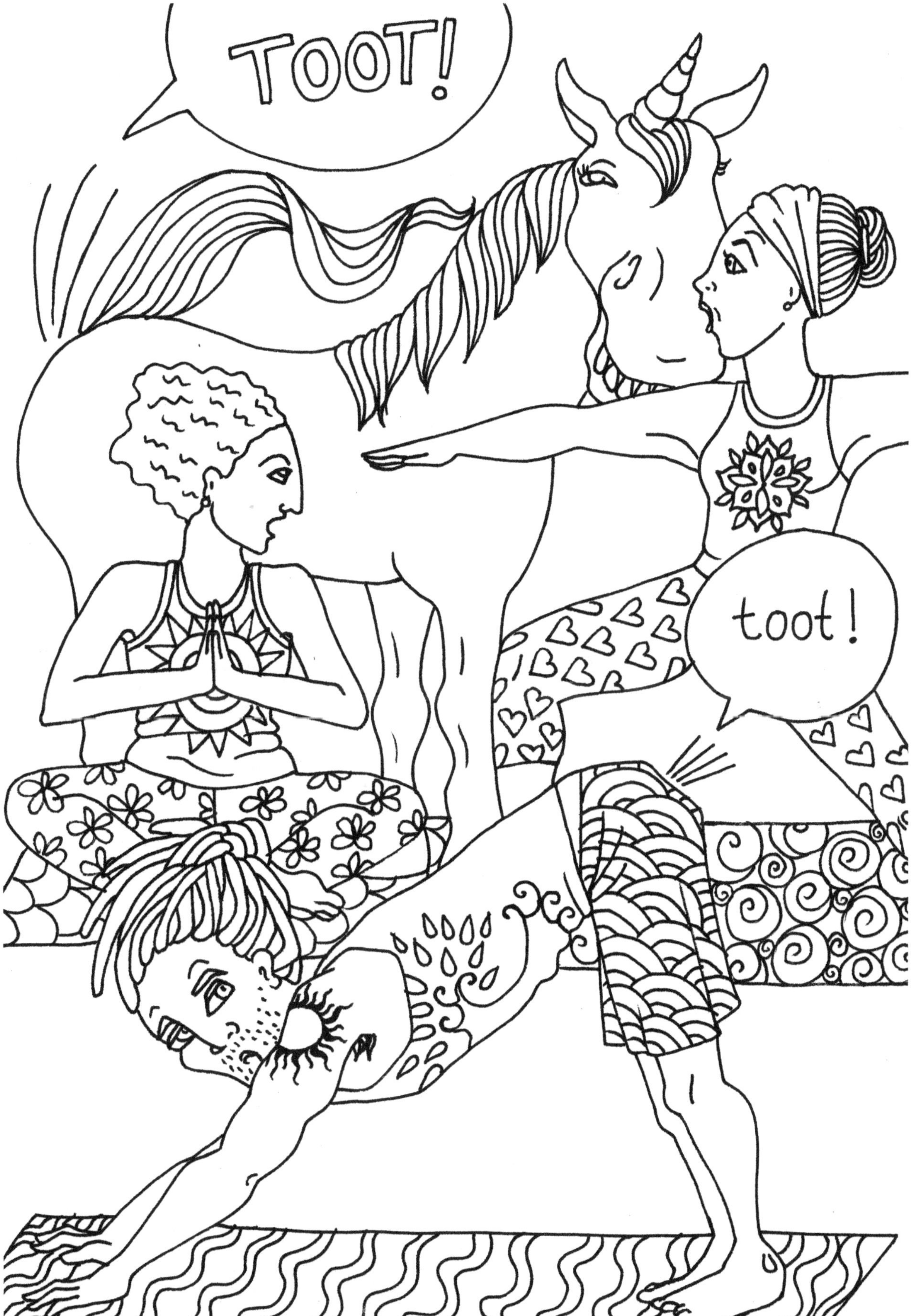
TOOT!
toot!

And look after you when you feel sick

Your unicorn will kick you up the bum when you need it most

the love Bar

Keep you away from your dodgy ex

Incoming call

Crazy Ex

Incoming call

Crazy Ex

Walk your dog when you're out of town

And never miss the chance to photobomb your friends

You'll always have a friend on the ferris wheel

Janny's
Fabulous
FERRIS
WHEEL

Fanny's Fabulous FERRIS WHEEL

And you'll never have to worry about your tax return again

TAX
AGENT

TAX
RETURN

TAX
AGENT

TAX
RETURN

Your unicorn will even help you beat the bully

Once you've found your unicorn, everything will be alright

Sketch and color testing zone

Sketch and color testing zone

Sketch and color testing zone

Sketch and color testing zone

www.ingramcontent.com/pod-product-compliance
Lightning Source LLC
Chambersburg PA
CBHW081222020426
42331CB00012B/3069